MW01093285

# MADAME X

# DARCIE DENNIGAN

# CANARIUM BOOKS
ANN ARBOR, BERKELEY, IOWA CITY

SPONSORED BY
THE UNIVERSITY OF MICHIGAN
CREATIVE WRITING PROGRAM

# MADAME X

Canarium Books
Ann Arbor, Berkeley, Iowa City
www.canariumbooks.org

The editors gratefully acknowledge the
University of Michigan Creative Writing Program
for editorial assistance and generous support.

Cover: Carl Dimitri, *Monk on Piano* (detail).
Mixed media on masonite, 2011.
Used courtesy of the artist.

Design: Gou Dao Niao

First Edition

Printed in the United States of America

ISBN 13: 978-0-9822376-8-7

# CONTENTS

"I  advance, pointing to my mask."

# THE YOUNGEST LIVING THING IN L.A.

The youngest living thing in L.A. was my baby.
The oldest living thing was the wind.

The wind grew well in that city in the desert.
As did my garden of well-tended cement.
As did my baby, whom I held like a heavy statuette.

I named him *Mill* at his birth ... *As the wheel goeth by drift of water* ...

And he grew and the wind blew and we lived in that desert and ...
no rain. No rain, no river. No sound of water. But for—

The fountain water.

The official fountain. Which flowed. Every day. Every day the
baby slept. The baby breathed. The fountain flowed. It flowed
imperceptibly. As if its water were fast asleep.

We stood on the fountain's shore: woman + newborn.
We made one totem.
I named the baby *Easter Island*.

We played I Spy.

I saw: coins at the fountain's bottom. Eyes. Copper cataracts, winking through the water at us.

I held the baby close. I held the baby stiffly. I brought the baby to see nobody.

I saw: statues in the fountain's water. Statues in tall grasses on the shore of a sea. I turned to tell somebody. The city had disappeared into complete silence. There was only: the baby.

We were watching the water wrinkle in the wind.
In the distance, maids were ironing.

Overhead: jets drew ciphers in the blue with their chalk.

*The drift of the maker is dark.*

*Beware that by the drifts thou perish not.*

The statues, the statues in the strange fountain were looking at us. They were weeping and turning, turning and weeping.

They might have seen the city shimmering in the sun and wind, and known ... It was a city with no one in it. If a door somewhere on the street opened, it would always be ... no one.

It would be a bad draft that had blossomed.

I longed for meadows white with drifts of snow. I named the baby *Drift*.

In the winter I had planned to bring him north. To a barn's eaves, to hear icicles drip. To prepare him to grow up in the path of the next great glacial drift.

City whose sky was white jet streaks.

Whose houses were apparitions of asbestos flakes.

Whose homeless sipped wind from tins.

Whose only water was the strange fountain.

*Angel, my angel, my sweetheart, wake up. See the foam on the wave, see the tornado, the hurricane.*

We stood on the fountain's shore. The wind blew particulates of rug powder, of lemon-scented floor polish. The maids of the city were cleaning so completely.

And mutely.

There may have been other names I gave the baby.

*Zeno sweet Zeno*

*Little fellow little fellow*

*Vertigo*

I said to the baby, We will stand here until there is snow on the mountain.

I may have meant to say *fountain*.

We peered all day into the strange fountain.

I said to myself, That is just your face stiffening around your cheeks. That is just grass growing at your feet.

I held the baby all the time, and he never ever cried.

# THE ATOLL

*Even the children, and the very little ones at that, did not die just any child's death; they pulled themselves together and died that which they already were, and that which they would have become* ... This and much more have we ... very fortuitously ... learned from the Atlanteans ... The Atlanteans ... it was all so very lucky ... We'd been testing fission ... fusion ... fission ... They were downwind ... just enough ... If the rain falls too lightly it's no good ... if too heavily ... obviously ... Upon the lovely dark-haired Atlanteans the rain fell just right ... ... ... *All Atlanteans*, we said over the loudspeaker ... *All Atlanteans must exit the island* ... They were nodding ... bowing ... Maybe politeness ... maybe vomiting ... We escorted them ... to a very nice ... resort-like ... laboratory ... Would you like another martini, we were heard to say ... frequently ... It turns out ... strontium loves ... it just loves bones ... and cesium-137 rests in the eyes ... and gamma rays go right to the blood ... And the miracle was ... we were hard-pressed to find a morbid ... process ... That is ... none of the Atlanteans made an untimely ... Yes there were lesions ... sorecuts ... Many of the men who'd been wearing shorts ... many of their ... And there were the usual number of miscarriages ... maybe a bit more ... but nothing too ... measurable ... But the children ... ! They were the most ... interesting ... Their skin ... it began turning ... not the gold of tans but of ... gold metal ... chemically elemental ... positively ductile ... And their teeth ... their teeth had turned ebony immediately ... But the amazing ... thing ... was the glowing ring around each bald kid head ...

*Dear Atlanteans we are sorry to inform you* ... But the

Atlanteans were ... smiling ... They ... thanked us ... patted our lab jackets ... Then they turned away from us ... They turned back to the children ... in the sand ... building castles ... and alphabets ... and ... grand frigates ... with sand yes ... but also with pieces of ... They were building pillars of ... bone ... they built a frieze ... with an image of the sun ... it was a sun the size of a heart ... a heart the size of the fist of a kid ... They were playing in the sand with their own skin and organs ... *Dear Atlanteans* ... We were genuinely sorry ... for the mistake ... and for what they had mistook ... Yet the Atlanteans ... such a gracious people ... One Atlantean father ... picking up a black tooth ... the tooth of a child ... He smiled ... and said ... with such solicitousness ... *Are you getting all this ... ?*

# THE CONTAMINANTS

*Because Nazi venom had seeped into our very thoughts, every true thought was a victory* ... Speaking of seepage ... Something had gotten into the water ... some kind of chemical ... poison ... or just the sun ... just the sun had got in and dried it all to bone ... The point was ... There was very little water ... Thus not the time ... to bring a baby into ... it all ... but I did ... and it was triplets ... three new babies ... and tribal fights over clean liquid ... well what do I do ... well I wanted to continue to be optimistic ... But was that true optimism ... or residue ... leftover ... from ... the commercials on pessimism ... As for nutrients ... they had looted the markets ... Wasn't it natural anyway to nurse ... but there were three of them ... an unnatural number ... and anyway nature ... There's enough cases of Coke in the root cellar ... but the militia has taken our straws ... the other militia, our medicine droppers ... dew in concave rocks ... ? well for that matter how about bowls ... bowls of dew for breakfast, sweet babies ... but the dew ... probably full of chemicals too ... yes ... and so it will be bean juice, juice from cans of beans ... Then they were sipping it ... ! Overjoyed, moved, to see their little mouths working the bean juice off my fingers ... It was all going to work out ... I took them for a walk ... Rigged a moving dolly into a pram ... proud ... optimistic ... be-lilac'd ... ! my triplets ... The number three has magical residue ... Was that my idea ... ? or did I overhear ...

But my bunker neighbors ... They said ... What kind of cruelty ... ! more babies ... ? That was what they said ... also the word *idiot* ... a lot ... The biggest bunker neighbor said ... It ... and it ... and it ... are what we cannot afford ... the methane from their baby gas alone ... I started nodding ... but I ... kept my own mind … The triplets were gurgling … They were so hearty … They would, when they learned to walk, stand very straight … they would invent it all anew … Barefoot may you forever be … I didn't have them for myself … Everyone'd been warning … Perpetuate the species … Don't … I wasn't a nazi for either … side … I had them for the sake of optimism … that was a true thought … that was a victory … Victory … I said it aloud … *Victory* was not the right word … it sounded like war … one side won and one side lost … What about the third baby?

# WHALE

He was nice and I was nice and when that is the case what to do but consolidate.

We bought a house.

In the years before we'd bought a house I had dreamt of a house and had loved dreaming of a house and then we had a house and I missed my dreams.

So I resumed them.

—The real estate agent stood on the lawn. She was my mother and she was also, in the dream, a large bird. It was a strange neighborhood, set deep in a valley. I kept asking my mother, the real estate agent, why the hills there were so blue but she kept trilling *Copper plumbing! school system!* and I knew she did not want me to know the answer.

—Out back was a deep well and we were rolling a rock over the grass to cover the well so that the kids would not fall in and the rock was very very heavy but in the dream I knew that, in real life, the rock was no bigger than my husband's eye.

I tried reading Jung.

On page one, there he was, wishing to remember only when the imperishable world irrupted into the transitory one.

I said *irrupted* aloud. Then slept.

—We were frozen in the yard of a dollhouse. The yard was turf instead of grass. I was the wife doll in a lounge chair. The husband figure had a rake in his hands. The kids were also dolls and there were bubbles around their doll heads and they were posed as if trying to pop them. Then the yard suddenly exploded and in my doll head I thought, *Run.* Then it was later and a toy boat was coming to collect our bodies from the scene.

—The real estate agent's throat was blocked. I knew that she had tried to swallow sperm and I knew that it was whale sperm. I was behind her in the Heimlich position and she took my arm from around her waist and pointed my pointer finger up at the sky where the sun was bright and high. I knew even during the dream why I was dreaming this and it was because, in real life, my mother has a high and bright voice.

—A homeless man was at the door of our house. It was my husband. I opened the door. He wasn't speaking. I spoke. Everything I said was sounding flat. In the dream I told myself, *Say something not flat, say something round*. I looked over the man's shoulders out at the round blue hills. I said, *Boo hoo*. I remember in the dream how glad I was that it was a dream because I had said the wrong thing.

The day after *that* dream, someone knocked on our real door.

I did not answer. I was pretending to read Kierkegaard.

A moment later my husband came in from the kitchen and asked me, *Who was that at the door?* And I said, *It was you.*

I said, *I think it was you.*

# THE SHOOTER

*When asked, if you say "I do not dance," the next day an infant is born without feet* ... That's what Sister Mary said ... Then yesterday my friend said that he heard the world is in the fourth stage ... that the fourth is our final ... our worst ... that the Dharma bull is standing on one hoof ... I said You're right ... And we both felt energized ... exultant even ... I turned on the news ... maybe meltdown ... maybe revolution ... We listened ... This fourth stage ... such science ... such ... fruit ... They interlace apricot with plum ... and the outcome ... ! Plus ... say they take you to the ICU ... if you get shot in the head ... if that happens ... they can use these tiny copper tools ... they can remove half your skull ... ... This was all mostly me talking but I guess I wasn't listening ... I was eating ...

It was a feast ... Kiwi abounded ... Kiwi ice sculptures ... Kiwi fondue ... Kiwi boats ... Kiwi fountains ... I heard my friend's voice ... He was saying ... *Kiwi* ... but with a lot of ... pain ... As if the kiwi were killing him ... I looked up from ... my trough ... His voice was coming from ... the radio ... ? There *was* a radio ... lodged in the kiwi gateau ... There was kiwi veal ... I'm sorry I said ... to the invisible host proffering the kiwi bacon ... I'm sorry ... I'm a vegetarian ... There was even ... now that I was looking ... encased in brown fur ... a kiwi person ... I'm sorry ... I can't ... Where was my friend ... He was so polite ... Even among cannibals ... If asked to eat children ... He would acquiesce ... He once told me ... he'd rather eat than dance ...

# THE DROUGHT

*Dip him in the river who loves water* ... said the cook on the cooking show ... Take the hearts of thirty ducks ... and here's the trick ... You must keep them wet ... the way to go ... the way to go is broth ... Okay ... Broth of hearts of duck ... I went to go buy broth stuff ... a bay leaf ... Oh said the grocer ... With duck heart what you want is spice ... Curry the thirty hearts he said ... Back home ... Hurrying ... Okay, curry ... The mailman smelled the place ... Oh ho, he said ... I smell blood ... he opened the pot ... Why if it isn't 30 duck hearts ... Of course you're going to skewer them ... ? Skewers ... I had to ... I had to go ... I ran down to the hardware depot ... Skewers ... ? Well it's not BBQ season ... I persisted ... I explained the meal ... the populace ... Meanwhile ... customers were coming ... buying out all the salt and shovels ... for the blizzard ... buying out all the fireworks ... for the Fourth ... buying out all the hammers and nails ... for Hurricane Ross ... Remained: some rope ... I'd hang them ... if I had to ... It's not thirty duck hearts is it ... asked the clerk ... I didn't dare talk ... To skewer the hearts of thirty duckers ... he said ... you need the beaks of thirty ivory-billed woodpeckers ... Are those ... rare? ... As rare as they come, he said ... Better give me 31 ...

Ran home ... the kitchen was smelling ... Okay ... Okay ... Almost ready ... The places set ... Candles lit ... The downstairs neighbor tuning her pipe organ ... ... 29 special guests filed in ... Please sit ... May I present ... In the heart of each duck ... there was a glint ... majestic ... They said, Is that ... ? Yes, I said ... Yes ... each one swimming in sauce and broth ... Oh, they said ... Oh no no no ... Had I ... ? Were they ... ? No, no no no no ... *Dip him in the river who loves water* ... Yes that's the recipe I followed ...

That's not the way it goes ... anymore ... they said ... They said ... each heart should be served raw ... and drowning ... in a sacred diamond-flavored fountain ... I was so ... I didn't usually believe in impressing ... But these guests! ... Honestly ... They were just ... They were as hungry as I was ... One especially kind ... one offered to ... to pawn the woodpecker skewers ... I lied ... said they were worthless ... said, Oh they were free ... Oh just papier-mâché ... Oh found a ton of them lying around ... down ... where the river used to be ...

# STRAWBERRY

We were at the French restaurant and the waiter approached with what looked like a plate of food, something or other. *Here, madame,* and by that he meant me, *is your plat.* Plat he said. Which was what we called a neighborhood laid out all in the same way. I grew up in a plat on one side of Wakefield Street. My friend Katie Callaghan grew up in a plat on the other side. I thanked the city planner who stood before my dinner table with his little model of trees and roofs and roadways arranged on his clean white disk and as he set down the plat I looked for the Callaghan manse. Now that I am thinking again of this story I am thinking that it must have been a story I *read.* Because *plat* the way the waiter must have said it and *plat* the way we said where we lived look the same but out loud I would never mistake a *plat du jour* for a working model of my old neighborhood nor of the nicer one of Katie Callaghan. Though I would possibly confuse the waiter's *plat* with the action of a story, which is maybe how this ... But before the plat, we'd been eating the appetizer, which the waiter had called *hors d'oeuvres,* which felt, after he announced it, compelling. As I chewed the first of these apps, I thought to ask the waiter, *But what is this?* And he said, *Straw*—and I said *Straw!* We used to have a goat, the only goat on the plat, and he slept on straw and sometimes when I was upset and didn't know it yet I would chew on a strand of his straw and it would taste like my memory in January of the smell of grass. Straw, however, is incomestible and this was meant to be a finer kind of restaurant, so I said so. *Oh no*, said the waiter, *No, I had definitely appended a berry to the straw. Very well*, I said. *That changes it.* If this appetizer he had given me, this order, was a strawberry, then I swallowed it five minutes ago. Then I must have strawberry strands in my teeth. My fingertips must have little stains of red juice. I touched my face, and I am always very pale, in disbelief.

# THE OTHER FOREST

*To insects — sensual lust* ... was how I began my talk ... On
Paradise ... at the local library ... It would be a nuns-only
audience ... I knew ... ! So I'd donned my habit ... wore a ton
of More Spirit Than Flesh make-up ... And ... brought props
... props in my large portable closet ... l'Armoire Secrète ...
Got to the library assembly room ... Fuck ... the one ... only
... person in the audience ... my husband ... Who ... I knew
... ! always preferred I get right to the ... Thus ... *Paradise
is sex sans bodies* ... *Paradise: Travesty* ... *Mechanical birds* ... *Exegetes*
... Was I losing ... ? Quickly to witticisms ... *I don't like sexing
but I love having sexed* ... The audience member ... the audience
member was ... demanding to see the inside ... of l'Armoire
Secrète ... Fuck ... I ... I began fumbling ... with the golden
lock ... Took a minute for nunly explication ... *Sex lubricates
... the locks on the gates* ... *Paradise-wise* ... When the Armoire
doors were ... I stepped aside ... let the audience member
... He got very close ... peered in ... put his whole head
... I regret he said ... he was nervous trying to joke ... I
regret I've forgotten my spelunking costume ... Shush I said ...
Keep looking ... Though really there was nothing to see ...
l'Armoire Secrète was empty ... Finally ... he stood ... squinting
in the library light ... he peered ... right at me ... Hey he said ...
he came very close ... This was how a naked marble statue felt ...
Hey he said ... gentle-wise ... Love ... he said ... Love it's me
don't you recognize ... Of course I did ... had ... But had to
pretend I did ... not ...

*Will the audience member please take his seat* ... I said it
resolutely ... though not ... firmly ... I began again ... *On Paradise*

... My voice as clean as the Dewey Decimal System ... I brought up my On Paradise PowerPoint ... visuals of forests ... trees ... He was seated ... Once my car broke down in front of a nunnery ... over the door of which was inscribed ... from Dante ...

*Nel mezzo del cammin di nostra vita*
*mi ritrovai per una selva oscura*

and I thought ... at the time ... I had been thinking *una selva oscura* ... had to mean dark self ... never bothering to ... the Italian ... I just ... plunged ... I'd donned a habit ... black robes ... ... Was I saying all this out loud ... or in my head ... ? It's hard to tell the difference ... if ... you talk enough ... *I donned these black robes and lived in shadows and* ... It was time for a rhetorical gesture ... Of course of course I said with a nod ... a nod magnanimous ... a nod sagacious ... a nod to a slide of particularly dark ... trees ... *Of course the wilderness spreads woe unto him ... who carries the wilderness with him* ... and the audience member ... I had him ... I knew ... Thus ... I parted my robes ... to show ... marching in and out of my cunt ... the ants ... Then ... the robes ... I shut ... He ... the audience ... was no longer standing ... very close ... Goodness ... ! I chided ... Such distance ...

# OUT OF THE ETHER

When two angels enjoy interpenetration, when there is a frantic
    fluttering then
falling back of wings, it's purely, *purely* a spiritual thing. So as
    many positions
as they tried, as much licking, they made no babies, no diseases—
    only hymns.


Oh to be a human!


*As to that corporeal light*, Augustine said—poor guy couldn't even
    sit,
like a good ascetic, primly and uncomfortably on a rock admiring
    a light rain in the sunset
for fear that his mind would be tempted away by an earthly
    beam …


The idea that light—that even light could breed desire …


That was why Angel A was leaving Heaven and heading to
    Los Angeles.
And Angel B, marvelous heavy with missing, thinketh that he will
    go there too,
get a one bedroom with a white rug and courtyard pool in Agoura
    Hills and Angel A woo.

They are right to come here. The neon is soft—mystical are the
    lights in the canyons—
and the ancient sequence of headlights creeping up the hill is—
    stirring.


*Transported I behold, transported touch—*


This is me typing—Darcie. I am a human.
At least, when I am not a monster, with boobs and mouth and
    fingers.


Oh angels, if I were Milton typing this, I would find you a way to
    have sex
that lets you be real, nipple-biting people—and also of one soul
    and holy and glorious.


Well, before you fell.


(Weren't all those bodies
found after Sunset Boulevard parties
with outstretched arms
face down in the blue pools
really amative angels
wings
in the chlorine already disintegrating … )

I'd say more, if this throat I have on earth weren't so thick with
   scars.
But angels, burns are *totally* worth the pleasure of giving a light
   saber a blow job.

# CATHOLIC SCHOOL REUNION

Remember how the nun said the last person to sleep with the Virgin Mary was Cervantes? We didn't do the math on the centuries. We believed her. *Yes, Sister.* Cervantes and the Virgin. There were connections. Like the house in Ephesus, the stone house, with a hearth and an apse, where the Virgin may have spent her last years. Through the bedroom window comes the sound of a stream. And on what might have been her bedside table is the book called *Don Quixote*. It is inscribed to Mary by its author, Cervantes: *And here, Virgin, is the child of my understanding.* We talked about it every day, taking up three seats at the very back of the bus. How the nun, who had never left Massachusetts, must have seen the house in a vision. How Cervantes was implying that Jesus was probably most definitely made from semen. But how we still—even more!—loved him. We talked about how the rhythm method didn't work. Talked about books. Late drives back after far-away games, we sang, with pointed exclamation, with high pitch, *To dream … the impossible dream … To fight … the unbeatable foe …*


Where could we hide a tattoo from the nun?

The hip.
The thigh.
The pelvic bone.


How has the nun still not died when we are all so incredibly old?

Mary and Cervantes on the mattress—

It is not a word for humor girls—

It means death, little death—

How many times do you have to before you're—

Dead?

Yes.

*No.*

From the bus's back window, I would behold—a dark field. In its very middle was a willow. Hanging from the bowing branches: post-suicidal crows. That looked just like heavy leaves, or just like a girl's clothes. And on the ground, with his back against the tree ... the sorrowful knight.

I heard he's dead.
I heard—

Me? What I've been up to?

Actually, tomorrow, I am traveling to Ephesus.
I too would like to imagine sex and have my own Jesus.

Of course, it's a different time. It's possible mine will have Styrofoam legs. A recycled aluminum-can cranium. No, I'm not wishing for a child in pain! I don't want any human to find himself through mortification. It's just—if we are going to have sex and then have children, real or not, I would like to write in the baby book something ... quixotic. So that when the child asks, *Where do I come from*, this can be the conversation:


—Where do I come from?

—Ephesus. It was late afternoon, on a straw mattress.

—Was it an August of incredible yearning? Was there, out the window, a stream murmuring?

—Yes.

—What came first, the stream or the yearning?

—*That* (I say with tenderness) is an inviolable secret, Jesus.


He is no longer listening. He is studying himself in the mirror. I would say he is eating his heart out but being imaginary, he has no heart, so he is eating his eyes out.

# THE DEBTOR

*Each joy still awaits us, but must find the bed empty, must be the only one, so that we come to it like a widower* ... That's what the tax form said ... I was being taxed ... abundance of joys I guess ... actually three ... two over the limit ... I felt fully guilty ... I looked out ... it's a crappy apartment ... but ... Sun a-peeking! ... Birds ... over the roofs ... hurtling! ... shit ... the view was on the verge of being a fourth ... Joy ... Someone knocked on the door ... Right when my mind was saying joy ... someone's ... I prayed it wasn't my landlord ... come to fix the stove ... the shower ... the light fixture ... But no ... It was the joy tax collector ... he was short ... Zaccheus-y ... with a little calculator where his left hand would be ... May I come in? ... I was uncertain ... What kind of payment ... Sir, is it money ... or ... do you exact ... tragedies? ... He was kind ... a kind joy tax collector ... explaining the system ... Everything must suck at once ... Except ... Do I get to choose ... I had a child so of course the choice ... He very kindly shook his head ... He asked for a glass of milk ... It was sweet ... It was sweet the way he drank that milk ... The way small boys do ... full of greed and then just ... full ... You see, he said ... putting the cup down ... burping ... you see how it's done ... Was he talking ... multi-tasking? Or ...

It was getting late ... At this time ... I was usually ... welcoming my child ... I was espousing ... then there'd be the mailman ... joys joys joys ... Where were ... Where ... Sir ... ? Sir ... ? Oh ... The joy tax collector was good at looking people straight in the eye ... Fine ... ... ... So was I ... I see, sir ... Oh I see ... It was time for me to kneel ... He anointed my forehead with his calculator ... Arise, arise now and go ... I went ... straight to the bed ... But the joy tax collector had taken the pillows ... the crumbs ... the dolls ... the books ... He had taken even the ... Okay, I said ... Okay the bed is empty ... I await my joy ... Oh, he said ... You misunderstood, he said ... You are the joy ... and I am ... the widower ... He said ... You must ask to see credentials next time ... You must never open ... to a stranger ...

# THE JOB INTERVIEW

Actually, my current one—in the sacristy—is a good job.
And you know, it's *fulfilling*?

The pay isn't great, and I've had to make accommodations.
Bring a lunch and all. But if I forget my sandwich, there's always
    extra ... bread lying around.

And wine.
Though on the job I would never!

Though, this is kind of gross, but—
I've acquired a bit of a taste for baptismal water.

After the water washes over the baby's forehead, you can't just
    dump it—
There's a special baptismal water sink, with a sacred drain.

Since it's so sacred—you know, the white lace, the whelp's skin—
Or maybe so dangerous—full of germs of original sin—

It seems a waste to put it down the drain.
So I've been sipping it.

Since I'm confessing, it'd probably be a stretch to say I only eat
    the communion bread in emergencies,
because I pretty much eat it all the time.

Though the incense under my arms was a singular occurrence.
I'd forgotten deodorant that morning, that's all.

That day, I may have performed my tasks in the sacristy a little
   more emphatically—
To, you know, get a little heat going under there.

The smell of the incense made me feel as if I were leading a
   solemn procession.
It also made me feel sort of sexy?

Anyway. I can't keep this job.
And I can't go back to the museum gig.

I mean, I still have the uniform and no one said anything *explicitly*
but after the incident with the Corot—

It was *The Boatman of Mortefontaine*—
Have you ever seen it?

It's not even really my taste.
If I were going to get caught making out with a painting I'd rather
   have had it be a Basquiat.

But.

There was something about that picture. It has autumn in it.
Even though the trees aren't orange or brown.

Actually, the trees are greenish white. The sky is white.
Every time I'd look at it, I'd feel white and blank.

And also the picture has this white and blank lake.
That I wanted to drink.


Later on, I did read about the pernicious effects of human saliva
    on paint.
It would be *terrible* to go back and see that I had caused any—


At one point, I also did some work as a skydiver.
It was a strange summer because I was pretty young and had
    just gotten my period.

Not to be gross, but I basically bled all summer. And that was
    mostly fine.
It was beautiful weather and I, you know, wore dark pants, took
    loads of baths.

But there was this one cloudy day, and they sent us up anyway.
I thought—if the crotch of my pants rubs against a cloud, I'll
    leave red streaks.

And I did fall through a cloudbank and even kind of tried to do a
    split mid-cloud.
But clouds are nothing to rub against, are nothing but emptiness.

I guess what I'm trying to say is that sky diving is still an option.

#1 I am not an idealist!
#2 I'll work anywhere and hard.

The thing with this sacristy job is—

The eating and drinking the bread and water is fulfilling
and I don't think anyone minds too much.

But part of the job is taking care of the vestments and once a week
    you need to iron them.
And they're long—these long, white robes with 80 million folds.

And forget trying to do it on an ironing board.
So I've been using the altar, because it's really just the right
    length.

Something about pushing the iron back and forth—
All that cheap white cloth—

The altar has saints' bones buried inside it—
In the afternoon there's the stupid beautiful light through the
    stained glass—

I don't believe in God though. That's not where this is going.

Even if I believed *the Word became flesh*, well—
I'd probably just want to have sex with it.

Because there I was, just vestment ironing!
My mind was blank.

And the altar and the space were so majestic.
And the part of me that really responds to majesty are my hips.

So I was sort of rubbing myself against the altar.
And obviously, having an orgasm is antithetical to the whole spirit
of the job.


I'm so sorry,
so sorry to have a body.

But how else.


I don't have heaven.
I don't have clouds even.


#3 What I'm really good at is loving this world well.


I just don't know who—
who I'm supposed to be or how to make enough money.

# THE REVOLUTION

*Don't be bored, don't be lazy, don't be trivial, and don't be proud* ... Okay baby ... ? He says to me ... Baby ... Sit down ... There was a bomb ... a bomb in a crowd ... one town over ... Oh ... I hadn't ... No you wouldn't have he says ... Because I'm so ... ? Because of the blackout ... They're blacking all the good news out ... ! He grabs my foot ... in ... fierceness ... But also please don't be too serious ... Hey I say ... today there was a bumper sticker ... Piping plovers taste like chicken ... But no chicken for him ... I know that ... still ... I like wings ... and eggs ... and snacks ... Run devil dogs run ... Now he's massaging my feet ... He believes in ... aliens ... historical ones ... that built the pyramids ... He believes it was not the Egyptians ... no ... their tools could not cut ... the basalt ... the granite ... and the tonnage ... he likes to say that ... the tonnage ... ! Don't be bananas, don't be lemons, don't be ... tangelo ... We are on the couch ... we turn on the radio ... The reporter's in ... the middle of ... she puts her cell phone up ... and from the mob ... a man's mouth ... comes out ... What is he saying ... ? This couch is the color of teargas and ... tangerines ... I would like to fall asleep ... mid-foot massage ... while sucking ... the juice from a coconut ... But ... but ... I know how it goes ...

*The slightest loss of attention leads to death* ... Oh yes yes I say to everyone ... I'm listening to you ... but only half ... Here he comes again ... Baby the radio ... they're saying ... a fruitman ... a fruitman lit himself ... on fire ... lit his fruit and his shoes and ... ... ... and all the fruit burned ... and him ... and afterward ... it was all just ash ... and mango ... the mangoes ... sitting there all pretty ... and still ... still chilled ... still juicy ... as if they'd been ... in air conditioning ... ... ... Oh ... Oh the radio ... they're always finding ... meaning ... No listen he says ... Listen ... But I just want to go ... Baby don't be proud he says ... But I don't ... I just ... Baby the mangoes ... the mangoes were cold ... you have to pay attention ... I don't care I don't care I know how it goes ...

# IN THE BAKERY

*for Tim*


It was in August, such a lovely summer, that I began the massacring. The flower killing. Feeding the sunflowers to the industrial dough mixer.

Soon there was enough yellow petal pulp for twelve loaves.

For twelve times ten loaves.

For twelve hundred loaves.


One of the food critics in town came around to inquire about my baking system.
… I glanced at the machete, propped next to the ovens.


Toward October (and what auburn weather!), I still felt *it*, the substance of the soul, the libidinal terrible whatever.

I sat out back with the two countergirls, Haley and Shayla. There was one cigarette, and we were sharing.

*Mourning is the horizon of all desire*, we were commiserating.


But Haley and Shayla, they're—

They sell Kaiser rolls and sliced Sicilian and then they leave and
put on a fancy tanktop and go out for the evening.

They go even though—

The little white clematis cling to the fences.

The blossoms of the clematis—

(At dawn the buds were dying as a sweet white bread was rising.)


November
How beautiful were the yellow mums in the thin wintry sun!
The bread they made had the hue of golden potatoes.


December
Specks of red in lit windows: amaryllis
that I stole and slaughtered and sold inside a *pain de mie* roll.


I love how in the cold, my breath flowers before me.

January, February
I hacked through the ice to get at flower fetuses. The breads were
very seedy.

Spring
It was really beginning.

Baguettes made entirely of white peonies.

Brioche from the blood of purple lilacs.

Long lines outside the bakery's door...


*What is the secret ingredient?*
I confessed: *Flower. Flowers! Please, put me away. I am desperate.*


Summer
I could not go through another.

The woodbine had barely begun and already the mornings were
full of the scent of them.


Not one honeysuckle would go unsucked—unless—


I closed the doors (every season is too full of longing!) and
rechristened myself Flora.
I drank a vat of rose water and put both my wrists through the
slicer.

And then I began to bleed—a white powder.
Flour.


And then you came in.
I would have known you even if you were not wearing in your
buttonhole a carnation.


*The bakery is closed*, I said tersely.
I was bleeding profusely.


I loved you even before you said
*Nothing breaks more slowly, more silently, than bread.*


With my blood pouring out as a fine, dry flour
let me confess before I expire.


There on the counter, in that vase
fresh and pink is the corsage I was keeping for our dance.

# WE HUMANS

My boyfriend believes aliens built the pyramids. He is very smart. I say to him, *You are the smartest person I know.*

We are in bed watching, on the laptop, the PBS special *Pyramids. Their mysteries, etc.* When he isn't in laughing throes, he is full of woe. *The truest of all men is the Man of Sorrows ...*

I hand him a typed-up fact: He worries it between his hands till paper roses pop out of his sleeves.

A bouquet: In the fall, the doorbell rang over and over unbidden the morning his mother was on her carpet dying. And the bell (he has the Italian way of making emphasis with his arms) does not have faulty wiring.

*Proletariat* must be one of his favorite words. Tonight I ate too many Oreos and referred to myself as *lumpenproletariat* but after he laughed he was not amused.

Atheism is lonely-making. In the dark of our apartment (he loves the Christmas tree but unplugs its lights), we feel the planetness of the planet. After the laptop glare has left our eyes, we will see from our window the stars, whose aliens make much more beautiful paper roses.

Who wants what is true, or woe? What I want is children.

# THE HALF-LIFE

*We won't have destroyed anything unless we destroy the ruins too* ... So when the nuclear holocaust happened yesterday, it was bad of course ... very bad ... for the world ... but we were still ... we of Bethany Home Hospice ... for us, it was ... As head nurse I went ... bed-to-bed ... giving the residents the ... message ... *Nuclear free-for-all* ... *world gone* ... *Bethany Home made of nuclear bunker materials* ... *constructed in the '90s* ... *when such things were* ... *on sale* ... *in short* ... We had survived and the residents were really ... roused ... The news ... the adrenaline ... their lives ... for months ... might be extended ... Clean drinking water wasn't a problem ... we had the IV drips ... also tuna, Jell-O ... enough rice pudding to fill a therapeutic whirlpool ... They got a knitting circle going ... tried their old hands at wool radiation suits ... they knit like crazy ... It was great to see their minds off their bodies ... But ... If we were what was left ... We would need to ... repopulate ... The early onset female dementias had to immediately start shock treatments ... in case their minds could make it ... if they became pregnant ... There were very few men ... there are always very few men ... but there were some male cases with sperm potential ... of course us staffers were mostly past child-bearing age ... but Bettina the night nurse's aid and Renaut the night security guy had been on a few breakfast dates ... our acutest hope ... They ... they were given the freshest cans of tuna ... Elvira on the third floor ... ninety and no help to ... Elvira said we could extract her healthy teeth ... for dental work ... if ever the new baby needed ... Really it was ... how it should ... all the dying ones feeling as if they were merely ... everyone putting in bids to have their deathbed be used for Bettina's labor ...

But then Bettina and Renaut had their baby ... and it was stillborn and ... Every single person who still had arms in Bethany Home took turns holding the ...

We will try again ... ! I said ... But Bettina and Renaut had ... as we were passing around their ... left ... to build a house of straw in the radioactive wilderness ... It was Helen's turn to hold the ... Helen had ALS and I had to help ... I was crouching down ... the infant half in my arms and half in Helen's ... Helen said How beautifully easy to break ... I said ... firmly ... Helen it is already broken ... But she ... she had meant ... me ... Then Filomena ... the blind diabetic ... rubbed my cheek and said it too ... So easy to break ... *That* ... I said ... is reality ... That's ... nature ... The seasons ... I said ... firmly ... There *are* four of them ... It *is* spring ... It was spring ... by the calendar ... at least ... I am not ... young ... autumn ... if anything ... but yes I've embroidered ... on my uniform ... peaseblossoms ... Please they said ... Filomena ... was fingering the threads ... of my peaseblossoms ... Please they said ... You could so easily ... break ... It was ... IS ... my job to ... make my patients comfortable ... Very well ... I slipped a thermometer from my breast pocket ... broke it ... sipped its liquid mercury ... a second thermometer ... third ... fourth ... Filled a clean bedpan with beads of liquid mercury and ate ... bibelot after bibelot ... But ... I continue to exist among them ...

# THE WAR

*Try as much as I can try not to be I, nevertheless, I would mind that so much* ... said the oats to the water ... which was working up to a boil ... See, I said ... to my daughter ... Even oats ... even oats maybe mind the boil ... mind becoming oatmeal ... For there was a small matter ... Oleg had sent me a letter ... I was to become ... under Oleg's orders ... an angel ... But we were late for school ... We should be frantically ... fossicking ... but no, not if I was ... dying ... always late ... I AM TO BECOME ... I announced to her ... before breakfast ... AN ANGEL PRESENCE ... I sugarcoated it ... an angel who will bread your house ... with lily dust ... Why would I need lily dust ... You'll know when you're an adult ... Oleg ... due any minute ... I was telling her how I'd be ... constantly ... crossing over ... to visit her ... She asked ... Will I know who you are? ... Well not at first ... No ... But I am sure you will always be gracious ... She was questioning things ... very ... worldlily ... which sounds like she was making the world's weight ... into a delicate petal ... of flower cellulose ... but no ... just ... worldly is what she is ...was ... Once ... when you were thirty-two ... and in that attic apartment ... and you ... well ... I understood ... And you were cold ... And I kissed your head ... The top of it ... In order to smell your hair ... Mom don't smell my head ... I'm not even eight yet ... Right ... Yes ...

I must have been having a nucleolytic episode ... in which I foresaw ... *Mom* ... I heard her ... I was still there but already ... in the ... underbelly ... ? I was thinking of a lovely girl I knew ... Last name De Flamand ... she once wrote a lovely piece ... about the word *daffodil* ... and the difference ...

between *yellow* and *yellowy* ... *Mom* ... How nice it was going to be ... to fit in ... the underneath ... or overhead ... what have you ... happily! ... It was all coming to a sharp point ... Had to get back to the present ... for a moment ... See ... I said to my daughter ... See ... Even oats mind becoming oatmeal ... We were staring down into the saucepan ... my daughter in my arms ... we played *Taps* ... on our lips ... in honor of the oats ... I was present for that peculiarly sad moment ... and still am ... afterward ...

# THE CENTER OF WORTHWHILE THINGS

Then there's the story of the two Costa Rican brothers. So close were they they cut each other's hair with closed eyes. Each, on his way to work, caught Frisbees the other had thrown amiss, years ago, on a different continent. They lived, in fact, leagues upon lengths away … the one on Guam and the other in Halifax Bay. No matter. Did it ever snow when they were young in Costa Rica? Does it snow in Central America? I don't think it does but it was writ on the dirt the day of their birth—the snowstorm. The snow—on Guam!—that filled the roads with miracles as one pedaled to the bakery, the snow in Halifax—not snow at all, an accumulation of little silverfish scales—as the other pedaled home from it. It was dusk on Guam, dawn in the fishing village. I do not know how the time in the story was so exactly parallel. I do not know how the same truck could have hit them both, how the same truck was both coming and going. The experts say that it was simply coincidence, that snow is dangerous, that neither wore helmets. When I stand citing statistics my friend walks in circles around me, 44 circles, because four, he says, is gentle and mystical and bakes pies. Dead center of the brothers' story there is, my friend says, something else. Maybe it is a magnet, dragged by the truck down the unpaved road, that wrote on the dirt of the brothers' birth. There is also their mother, confectionary sugar on her chest and shoulders, who baked white pies, she called them snowflake pies, she was famous for years for them, who, after the statisticians had had their say, baked 44 of these snowflake pies, and set them on 44 windowsills, and after they had cooled, she set out in the middle of the night, to feed the pies to each of us who had said that the lives of her boys made no sense. Who had said of the snow, coincidence.

# THE CORPUS

*The thing sought is in the seeking that seeks it* ... I sought to be an artist ... So I went to school ... *A* in all my classes ... I went on ... Wanted the *summa cum laude* next to my name in the art school graduation program ... I asked the school how to ... They presented three honors tracks ... suicide ... jail ... madness ... Madness was graded on a curve ... madness being ... relative ... The other two ... strictly by the book ... Okay I said ... Jail sounds good ... Alright then, they said ... We'll assign you an artist mentor ... who will stealthily note your ... progress ... A mentor who will reveal himself ... when you have ... passed your tests ... Thanks I said ... The art school had really thought of ... even suggested moving ... to Syria ... or China ... to up my chances for ... arrest ... but I liked the challenge ... the grandeur ... of America ... Arrest here ... almost impossible art-wise ... ! But I was driven ... driving ... My first installment ... "And the Hirsute of Happiness ... " ... was hairy ... ladders made of hair ... the hair of camels and weasels ... woven into ... ladder rungs and hung from the roofs of each branch of the Bank of the U.S. ... the hairy rungs blocked the doors to the ATMs ... I hoped ... I'd been hoping ... the customers would climb them ... But ... the branch managers brought in high-powered ... blowdryers and ... no one took ... of my work ... much ...

Until "Milkshake ... " which was just ... ice cream and Red Dye #3 ... ingredients in ... in crystal glasses ... that I sold only atop Mount Everest ... sold only to those ladies and gentlemen who could afford ... to send ... servants who ostensibly retained dignity ... during the hike up and back ... The milkshakes of "Milkshake" were ... many things at once ... a symbol of ... Also poisonous ... Jail was ... famous ... and I too was ... No one knew much of my ... conditions ... there was much ... torture ... etc. ... Years on end ... Then my final report card from art school came ... *F* ... All *F*'s ...

F in the thing thought is in the thinking that thinks it
F in the thing bought is in the thinging that things it
F in the thing taught is in the torture that brings it
F in the sing sought is in the wringing that rings it

How had ... ? The school knew then that I wasn't ... pure ... ? But they had set me on the track themselves ... ! The track itself was a trap ... The whole art school was a ... joke ... But only the school knew ... *that* ... only the school knew itself ... to be ... a joke ... The school had made me exactly what I ... and everyone saw me as ... except them ... it was their ... their little inescapable ... trapezoid ... I went mad ... I went back to my cell ... took a shard of mirror ... killed myself ... As I was bleeding ... my mentor came in ... beret and all ... right away I recognized him ... He said ... with compassion ... We at the school would be happy to grant you ... an aesthete's ... funeral ...

# IN THE AVIARY

Then I was trying to get me to a nunnery
but wound up at an aviary …

I rapped on the wrought-iron gates
till the shadow of a great wingspan darkened my face

With my belongings strewn like offerings
with, in my gullet, the word *salvation* stuck

I kneeled
*Oh Bird Superior*

And the Bird Superior pointed to the stone ground
and said, *Take a swan dive*

She said
*Pluck each feather from your body until you get naked and cold and die*

(These things are meant to break me but I think—I think they'll
salvage me)


In the real world I don't trust me in the spring with a robin's egg
The blue is so babyish and the shell so like a Chiclet

If I thought about it, I'd eat every blue oval, so I never, ever think
about it

But in the aviary … oh, in the aviary

I made myself hollow-boned
so his arms would definitely break me

I called and called and took
all my songs outside their parentheses


If you want a note to last, you have to hold it

Gingerly, I held the beak closed
I cupped the air around his throat

I'll be gentle, nightingale, if you'll let me dismantle
the words I've misheard

*Salvation* was not the Latin greeting
hey, you've come back for me

nor did *nightingale* signal a dark, strong storm
… except in me, in the aviary


Today *aviary* is just a *V* in the air of geese—
Autumn, and the light almost gone

Dark splotches of kids in the distance at the park
Soon their hands too cold to throw stones

Outside the aviary, isn't it always bird winter?
Bare trees, all the pulse migrated south …

But those who can take that quiet
can brush feathers with a small family around the fire


(I've almost ended there. Almost ready for my dive—)


Still, I need to tell
the tiniest shard of a story's eggshell

*how without words his fingers took the worm from hers*

I whisper this every time I want to hurt
It's exactly the quickened birdheart I came here for



I'm so sorry, robins, for eating your eggs
I am

But isn't that—I mean, I was wrong but—
I hope your loss means you will sing better songs

# THE MATRIARCHY

*A commitment to innovation qua innovation presupposes an investment in lineage* ... and let's be honest ... there is a feeling among many male Pietàs that their work will not matter in the scheme of art history ... For centuries men have been viewed as motherhood's ... antithesis ... I myself am a Pietà ... who happens to be ... male ... and I ... well it's a daunting task ... taking a men-inistic perspective when I am an artist ... I bristle at the very presence of *male* and *Pietà* in the same sentence ... And so ... now that I am asked for my response to the Madame's famous ... "Why Have There Been No Great Male Pietàs ... ?" I am reminded of the time ... years ago ... when I was at a party ... one of the rowdy Sistine Chapel ones they used to throw in the '70s ... talking to Ryan Flaherty ... who was at the time bringing his own Pietà poses to ... the inevitable ... and Ryan and I were talking ... and a woman came up and said ... What do you male Pietàs think ... ? Ryan grabbed my arm ... said to me Mitch ... he said ... *Let's get the hell out of here ... ... That* ... was my first response to Madame X ... Then I became curious about what a *woman's* response would be ... Parsippany thought it a travesty ... Dana said travesty ... too ... Laura ... who though dead ... said to me through her work that the question ... was an offense ... ! Against ... virgin motherhood *as a human generalness* ... and an offense ... ! against the maternal identity of ... men ...

... Rereading my response I see ... I've canvassed women ... Telling ... ? Not at all ... ! As if a chorus of female opinion were a prerequisite to knowing my ... It just happens that some of the most exciting ... I mean ... the long line of great Pietà advancements in the 20th ... I mean ... the Virgin laughing over

Christ's body ... the Virgin mourning Christ as a miscarriage ... the bitch Virgin holding Christ between her teeth by the nape of his neck ... the Virgin who left to find herself ... so many variations on the pierced milk ducts Virgin ... women ... all women ... This is not to deny my own ... my own work ... has ... greatness ... And I owe it to my own work to ... I owe other male Pietàs ... nothing ... I owe it to my own ... to work from within ... Men can't be mothers ... they say ... But my newest Pietà pose ... I look at the onlookers ... square on ... knuckles white ... tight ... I hold the Christ away from the camera ... for the better protection of ... my ... possession ...

# THE END IS NEAR

I said: *I wish I were the mother of poor, black men.*
I said it in a city all of a sudden strange, on a night of no moon, as I
    was driving through

because cars are wombs, because there was a moment
I dared to. *Look out for that moment* I will say now, to the self who
    drove

with no headlights or streetlamps or moon, who headed for
a square of light over the gas station's island

where a lone attendant was filling tank after tank, for we were all
    fleeing
and the baby and I were next in line. But as I turned to check on
    the baby I saw

the gas attendant's face staring at me through the passenger
    window.
*Hi there*, I said.

He—the gas attendant—nodded.
That nod! It seemed full of wise bruises and his eyes impossibly wet.

His face was not unlike my baby's, whose expressions I have often
    mistaken
for a poor man's.

The sweet thing is small enough to drift through a storm drain
or fit in a boy's already crowded fist

and smallness somehow equates with sadness.
But the gas attendant? No, it was the pity making him small, and a
   step before small

making it all
sad.

\*\*\*

There is the loneliness of babies and the loneliness of
the last gas station attendant in bad weather.

On that night, in the gentlest of whispers so as not to wake the
   baby in back,
I, my real self, nervously asked the attendant, What will you do?

He bellowed: *I am a poet*
and thus gained the upper hand.

*How beautiful the universe is!*
I ventured.

For a time, we watched my baby's tears sail silently through the
   night.
Then the lights on the gas station island switched off.

*The night completed its nigrescence.*
Which of us said that?

*Sir*, I asked, *where does the word* night *come from?*
*Is it related to other black things?*

But the baby chose this moment for his first utterance.
*Nigh*, he bleated. *Nigh. Nigh. Nigh.*

\*\*\*

The end is near. This story galls everyone I tell it to.
(Least of all because it describes not a friendship but an *encounter*.)

But it was so intimate! We were surrounded by dark cars rocking
    and bobbing
on the waters, and we, the gas attendant and I, were so close and
    lonely.

When you sleep in bed with a new baby in your arms—that kind
    of loneliness.
Everything is the baby, the bedroom is the end of the world,

but when the baby is calm you cannot know its mind, and you
    must
hold in your arms a strange thing.

# THE EXISTENTIALIST

*My kingdom, my kingdom for a* _____ ... For a what ... ? ...
I forgot ... I'm on the bus ... Now boarding: two Columbine-ish
kids ... with duffles ... In three miles we'll be at the bridge ...
The kids look relaxed ... but ... Calculate the risk ... Risk of two
long-haired trenchcoat kids blowing up this bus on the bridge ...
equals ... no is less than ... the risk of twenty short-haired men
... in khakis... blowing up a ... a ... transport ... or more than
the risk of ... one man ... in baseball cap ... blowing up only ...
himself ... Or not that ... That's stupid ... It ... If I die on this
bus ... well then ... I chose it ... Like last night in the library ... I
was talking to my friend ... loudly ... about the Augustine story
... Augustine going into the garden ... hearing the child ... crying
... I forget what ... Maybe crying Now ... ! or ... Check the book
... ! I don't ... but he checks the book ... he opens the book
blindly ... puts his finger on a ... at random ... at random he
thinks ... ! and lo and ... his revelation ... No more sex ... Only
God ... Augustine thinks it a ... miracle ... but ...

Okay why does the Columbiney kid have his hand in his
breast pock ... ? Okay anyway ... Aug. chose it ... the child was
probably crying Broccoli ... the freaking book probably always
falls open to that page because ... who's always reading it ...
creasing it ... who owns that book in the first place ... Nothing
... is what my friend said to that ... story ... Celine says *All
kingdoms end in a dream* ... I like that but that is not ... or
else it's too much ... Now the other kid ... unzipping the duffle
... Two miles to ... Well if ... I chose it ... The kids' hair in their
faces ... messy inside messianic ... When my hair stood up on my
forearm ... before anything bad had ... horror inside horripilation

... When Augustine ... in the throes of ... heard someone inside the party ask for ... a glass of water ... he wept ... What did he think he heard ... a class of laughter ... a gloss of slaughter ... The phrases must sound the same in ... was it Latin ... ? One mile to bridge ... My kingdom ... My kingdom for ... a horse ... Of course ... My kingdom for a horse ... Ha that's ... Last night I dreamt ... maybe this is a sign too ... I dreamt ... a terrible swift God ... was in my driveway ... I kept telling him to go away ... I kept saying Okay okay yes you're God ... but only because you're in the *style* of one ... I don't know why I said that ... in the dream ... he didn't have a God face ... but he had the clothes ... the Godly robes ... He was blocking my driveway ... This morning I chose ... to ride the bus ... And ... to ... not get off ... The boots of these kids ... these kids who maybe have guns ... bombs ... Are the kids' boots supposed to be the horses' hooves ... ? And then what is ... What ... Who is ... Who is riding ... whom ...

# HIGH AND BRIGHT AND FINE AND *ICE*

When the motorboat man asked me to love him

I whispered *precipice*
the word for the no-more-boyfriend feeling

because *precipice* contains *ice* (practically twice)
because I wanted teetering—

*What?* he said
*Yes*

His ears from the engines—so hard of hearing—his hands always
   so hot

Mid our first winter—I'd clung so long to the dock
he had to crowbar my fingers off

Each digit cracked so cleanly
Would you say they break like *icicles*? I asked sweetly

I knew I was nothing! But if I could sustain one song—
*I is, I is, I is I is I is*

I could be: *ice*

Sex on the bathroom's cold marble counter was best
I whispered *statuette, monument*

*What?* he, sculpting my legs, said

*Yes*


The child? I named her *Cecily*
It sounded like *iced lily*


For pure, I said *pristine*
At the ocean, I said *brine*

*Isle* for vacation; for flowers, *edelweiss*

But when I said (only of late, late!) *I choose ice*
Brittle pearls broke behind my syllables

Did he hear me?
Again, twice, thrice:

For my love
we would need to live
in a great pyramid
We would need to sleep
beneath the continental shelf
with Antarctic crust blanketing us
The only driveway to any kind of house

is an iceberg-ridden Northwest Passage
When I whispered *universe*
you were to translate it as
*one bright line*
*one bright rime*

# "ILS SONT DANS LE VRAI!"

I hear imaginary news on the radio all the time now. I heard the other day:

"Deep field researchers have found a meadow of what looks like diaphanous tulips but what is really"

—and then I moved out of earshot of my daydream.

This morning I heard:

"A rare strain of seahorses, 1,216 specimens, found beneath Antarctica's continental shelf."

I typed this information into a search engine and—nothing.

But it reminded me of a dream I'd had while asleep, about seahorses the size of landhorses bobbing along the North Shore. And the lifeguard at that beach blew his whistle and said "Everybody out of the water!" People were thinking *shark*. From where I was on the pavilion, I knew it was seahorses.

But the lifeguard was seeing not seahorses but torsos. He was frantic, jumping up and down on his platform, blowing his whistle:

"Everybody out of that water! It's the Archaic Torsos of Apollo!"

He got out his megaphone and said the whole poem, the whole thing, and I'll say it for you here now but I'll hurry it up …

*We cannot know his legendary head*
*with eyes like ripening fruit. And yet his torso*
*is still suffused with brilliance from inside,*
*like a lamp, in which his gaze, now turned to low,*

*gleams etc.                              Otherwise*
*the curved breast could not (etc. etc.) nor could*
*lalalala                     placid hips and thighs*
*to that dark center where (etc. etc.)*

*…………… stone ………… defaced*
*(tatatatatatatata)*
*wild beast's fur:*

*(etc.) (picking it up again now)*

*for here there is no place*
*that does not see you. You must change your life.*

The lifeguard. He was so young. I felt in the dream, this kid, this kid, he is so young he doesn't know sculpture from fish.

He was so full of feeling watching these broken Apollos wash in. I could see him mouthing
"You must change your life."

And you know what teenagers, real ones, do in these situations.

He scoured the shore for a horseshoe crab shell and broke off the long, straight, rigid tail. He sharpened it on some rocks. Then he used it like a sword, to decapitate himself.

# MATRILINEAL

My mother was a voluptuary. After secretary school she went back to stay with my grandmother in the house on the corner.

She came out only when my grandmother sent her for milk, for cigarettes, for wine biscuits and pizza strips.

No matter. She got offers.
Frank Lafazia loved her. And Matt McDonough. She wanted only my father.

He was the guy who stood inside the knight's armor down at the grocery. It was the Round Table Market, now out of business. They had the knight's armor by the door, for decoration.

My mother would come home with rust stains on her blouse, little bits of blood on her mouth.

My grandmother tried wicked tonics to cure her.
What's in there besides nothing, she'd yell at her daughter.

Not that my grandmother was much better.
Commandant of the local dead letter office. In charge of letters to toothfairies and deities. In service of the nonexistent address, she daily donned her postal cap.

So that was my grandmother. Sappho was the patron saint of our mophouse. The poet famous for poems that are not really, anymore, existing.

Every ancient unearthed papyrus roll Sappho wrote on has holes just about. Sometimes out of a whole poem just a few words have survived. Like, *Garlands of celery*.

Out of respect, we often bought these at the grocery.

I was older and had left home and the congeries of toast and butter winters when an ass in Cypress unearthed an intact papyrus.

A whole work by Sappho from the start to end.

When that papyrus came to town four years later, to a museum, I was right in line—

I waited hours to see it, and when it was my turn I sprayed balsamic vinegar on it.

If I ever have a daughter—by prisonguard or conjugal visit—

I'll name her Arc of a Circle. Or Ellipsis.

Or Awry By Any Means Necessary.

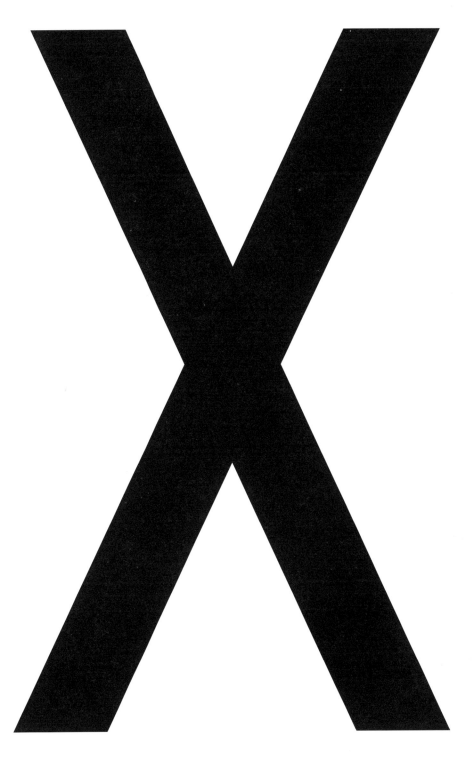

# SOME ANTICS

I am at Macy's looking for an honest clause.
They have only words.

The saleslady brings this one out from the back:
*There was a man who named his child Fetter, for he knew he'd be tied down*
*forever.*
*Six months later, the child had been abandoned.*

I add *Fetter* to our list and leave the wedding registry desk.


He gives me twelve red roses.
What do they mean?
My love, what do you think they mean?

When I think of roses, nothing stems to mind.


Honeymoon in Florida.
Breakfast in an orange grove with famous recluse lexicographer
Laura.
Over OJ, we all say nothing.

Three empty glasses and Laura finally says, Skin & bones.
What? my new husband says.
I whip at him, Shush! We are starving the language.

The *anatomy of truth*, I say to her. Yes, yes, okay!

Laura says, Don't say okay. You don't know okay. You are mishearing the signs.
Okay.

Dear, what shall our car bumper motto be?
*Peace?*
Not quite right.
What do you suggest?
*War is not the answer?*
Isn't that the same as peace?
No. Clearly peace is not the answer either.
But—
But—

Knock knock.
Who's there?
Any.
Any who?
Anyhoo, let's go on.

Tell me again why we had to name the dog Bartleby?
Because he prefers not to do tricks.
He won't even bark at other dogs. Is barking a trick?
The dog says a crowd is untruth.

When the honest word eludes, try to substitute.

I substituted *porridge* for *marriage*.
On all household documents, tax forms, what have you.
The boiling down, the grayness, and yes, the fortification—more
accurate.

For *child*, substituted *held*.
My held.

For she was, and she was and she was.
Are you hearing *hell* in there? I am not. There is a degree of
viseness that is quite agreeable.

My held.
Called it, during the fetus stage, *to hold*.

And so on.

I prefer *and so on* to *etcetera*.
The latter goes by too quickly to convey *sub specie aeternitatis* with
accuracy.
And fails to suggest hope of an end. If you trip over *and so on* you'll
get *soon*.


Why don't you ever say I love you?
I have endearment demophobia.
Why don't you like it when I say it to you?

You have endearment agoraphobia.

I wish we could shut ourselves up in a closet together.


Great Aunt Eileen, in a codicil to her will, left me a gift uxorial.
It's for when he wants to and I'd prefer not to.
It was her favorite word: *in-effable*.


Tell me again why we had to name the dog Bartleby?
Those mild eyes of his make me want to kick him.

I meant to say kiss him.

You have done both.
I have done both.


What did one tea bag say to the other tea bag?
The kettle's a-boil! We must, we must du-ty.


There is a vast unwritten clause—that I race and pound to—that I
palpitate to—
My belief in that vast unwritten clause brought it into being.

Well, what is it?
Well, it's a low talker. I can't quite hear it.

Knock knock.
Who's there?
(muffled muttering)
Who? Who?
Exactly.


I think often of little Fetter out there.
To be able to accurately answer *Fetter* to any number of questions.


We must, we must do tea.

Friends, I cannot entertain you eternally.
The knocking, the ringing and dinging, grow louder.
I want to go where the lemons taste like orange juice.


We must, we must du-ty.

Can I be honest?
*You* are that abandoned baby named for chains?
Maybe. Maybe not.
*Maybe* is awash in wishwashiness.
Fine. Either / Or.


*No more.*

*What is the reason?*
*Do you not see the reason for yourself?*


I want to hold my held.


Do not think that I do not believe in marriage.
I have read somewhere of a fabled porridge, of oats mixed with silver leaf.
And the eaters of this porridge live all their days shitting lovely silvery piles of luminosity.


I want to go where people say the sea is green.
*Is* the sea green there?
No. But their language has no word for blue.
Would you have loved me there?
Maybe. If they had a different verb.


Why did our goddamn dog never bark?
That wasn't his response to the world.
What was his response?
To lie down.

That was mine too. I put my lie down all over the house. *I love you. Yes. Oh yes. Yes, why not. And so on.*

# THE SPEECHMAKER

*I have no conception of the amount of succor that is being constantly used up* ... I declared to the press at the conference ... making sure to be ... exclamatory ... *Succor* ... *! Constantly* ... *!* I ... but my opponent ... he was saying at his press conference *Death* ... *! Death is the lens through which I see everything* ... How to contend with his ... gravitas ... ? Brainstorming session: Marv and I deciding ... Work all the succor angles ... Rep. X can have his death lens ... Succor ... What it even meant, half would, half wouldn't ... But then the press ... asking for specifics ... How much succor were we in debt for ... ? Then the networks picking it up ... Reliance on Chinese succor ... Russian succor ... succor from the Bengalese ... So they were going with steel ... or was it plastic ... ? *Succor* ... *!* I declared ... it ... There were runs on the bank ... *Succor* ... *!* dramatic dips on Wall Street ... *Succor* ... *!* All the markets raided for milk ... *Succor* ... *!* But then Rep. X was picking up on it ... saying ... *Rationing of succor needs to happen ... and it needs to start with children* ... It was ... shocking ... What was he ... ? I called my own conference ... *Succor* ... *!* How? The press demanded ... Marv had allotted me only three words at this particular ... I'd already said Hello ... How... ? *Baby jails* ... Baby jails ... Horrific ... Why had I ... I hadn't meant ... *!* Succor was ... That was not it ...

But the press loved it ... I was ... expert ... all the credibility I'd always ... I was asked to speak at Rutgers ... This was it ... This was what it ... took ... All the right people ... at state of the state banquets ... I admit ... I loved it ... loved ... careful to always hardly say ... lest someone ... Then one day a district road crew ... drilling ... hit an underground river ... a newfound river beneath the district ... I christened it ... The Succor River ... At the ceremony I brandished a silver dipping cup ... Filled the cup with water from the river ... and drank ... It was so cold and ... It was extravagant ... that river water ... I knelt ... put my mouth right in and ... How much did I drink ... ? I have no conception of the amount ...

# THE NINTH ANNUAL MEETING OF THE FRATERNAL DISORDER OF HISTORIC LINGUISTS

## OR

## THE ERROR OF MY MAZE

We lie in every word.
Did I say *word*? Oh dear. I meant *mode*.
We lie in every mode.

And not our fault!

My first utterance was a sentence ...

There was I, with my parents, in a forest, beneath our planet's one satellite, saying, *Look it's a full womb.*
They were good people, always uneasy. So they laughed.

How could they have known that elsewhere linguists were busy documenting the socio-spatial forensics of the M-W swap?

It wasn't until I went to university, until Edith Hamilton's *Witchology*, that I understood the ancient psychological crosspinnings of *moon* and *womb*.

My Dear Fellows of Indo-European Tongues,

As we start our symposium today, think for a second about our progress restoring the correct consonant to scores of syllables *wis*-heard since the Tower of Babel's ceiling fans stirred *M* and *W* into topsiturvitude ... Just this morning, the headline!

THE TRUE NATURE OF EENE MEENEE MAINEE MO REVEALED

*Not* a child's rhyme on the frivolity of choice, no, no—but a dangerous seven syllables on the woe borne from the liberty of hem hawing. The *Times* puts it thus, and I quote, "in *wavering* we all of course hear *moving*."

Yes, we're still having some troubles figuring out how to tell *Wuthers United*—who of course prefer the error *Mothers United*— and yes, pronouns and prepositions are proving profoundly ... heh.

I think though, friends, that the marled is coming around!

The recent decree out of Vatican City is a sign. *Blessed is the fruit of thy moon, Jesus.* Of course this begs the question: What to do about *Mary*? Yes, *Wary* does seem right for her, only how to convince others? And what, what to do about man/woman? It's tangled. I am not lacking hope. I received from a layperson just last Tuesday this letter and its linguistics of love spurs me on. The young lady writes,

*Dear Sir,*

*I am writing either to thank you or blame you for my lovelife. Really, I'm not sure what to say if anything at all. I do not know that the mouth has worth. You may interpret this as me saying* I do not know what was worth his mouth. *Both are true.*

*See, I was interning in a furniture store, tasked with rearranging the*
*showroom floor.*
*I put the divans to the east, the settees to the west. Couches north and*
*sofas south.*

*Except—*
*the divans were where the door was.*

*The manager was in a slight stew. He said, the door is impassable, to put*
*it wildly.*

*Yes, wild! I had thought then. You must understand, after such a*
*couchlife, how I longed to hear—*

*I think I love you, I said, to put it mildly.*

*The manager demanded, Who are you?*
*I was an internee. Who was he?*

*I am the widower, he said.*

*You must understand my mishearing. (Why wis-hearing?)*

*After he had had me, and I he, on the settee,*
*he spoke softly: Your body is the land of whelk and honey.*

*He repeated,          Whelk          and          honey.*

*Dear Sir, Sea slugs!*

*If he could have, with his tattered furniture fingers, traced across my shoulders* M I L K—
*Sir, do you have a provision for things such as these?*

*For he did not spell on my shoulders. He kneeled on his knee.*
*He said, Weary me.*

*I did.*

*I regret, sir, not swimming with him in the cold blue sea.*
*For I know you are thinking I don't know this, but I do. I know, or knew—*
*that what I had taken for the male wink*
*was really the lovely shuttering eye of a whale, a minke.*

*The story is slight. I know. It is ever so slight and meek, dry, barely palatable. But! It is wine.*

*Yours, in a sad wood, lost in the moods—*


Etc. etc.
She signs it very fondly, she sees the problems yet she also sees how the solutions are within our grasp.

These are mighty weighty times and I am simply glad to be a part of them.
I am spurred on.

# FUNERAL FOR A WALLFLOWER

~*Did you know her, No did you, No, You, No, I've come out of love for shy flora.*~

I've come out of a house with a cracked foundation and weeds come out of its cracks and what came out of me looking in the plant dictionary was discovering a wallflower was one of those weeds.

A real wallflower.
And then my landlord killed her.

The priest to me: Will you give the eulogy?
Me: Yes, but I am soft-spoken.

He doesn't hear me so I must start talking.

"She was born, dear friends, with a caul."

(The congregation thinks I said *pall*.)

"As a bud in the garden she met a bee, lately from Germany, who said to her *I have had a strange träume* and then touched his thorax, where his heart would be."

(*Dream* is what the congregation heard, which is of course not the German word for wound at all.)

The congregation! They are all crying.

"Listen. I'm sorry. Listen.
The petal of my tongue keeps slipping.
It does so often."

"When I was young and in school, I bragged, as I'd heard my father do, to the children.

I bragged, *We have a great store of wheat in our granary*.
But when I got home listen to what I had caused:

My father crying: *We are now poor. Our stores are empty. I went to fill the sacks and out flew wheat-colored canaries*."

I keep hoping you will interrupt me.

"But to return to the wallflower—

She was all stamen and skinnily elegant leaves. She was proud of her silken-haired seed crates. And she was very French and would call her seams her *siliques*.


What is the French for a wallflower vowing, *I will never come out of my secrets?*"


~*Did you ever smell her, No did you, No, You, Yes, her scent was nothing.*~


"Once, when I was at the cardiologist's, he sighed. He had been reading the EKG machine.

Me: Tell me please!
He: A fragrant cloudiness covers all things.

(silence)

He: What I smell is a heart murmur.
Me: It is the flower."


I keep hoping you will interrupt me.


"Personally I never want to live in a world where flowers are so precious we can't pick them. When I was young we had a tree that flowered pink for only a few days. And on those days we would tramp the flowers into the ground until they were dirty in the same way that months later the snow would be."


I keep hoping you will interrupt me.


"The flower broke every silence by saying: *I keep hoping you will interrupt me.*"


~*What did she mean, I don't know, Do you, No I don't, No I don't.*~


I keep hoping you will interrupt me is a funny thing to say but I think it is begging, in a way.


I think it has something to do with asking to be broken but I have as yet myself never had an interruption.

# ACKNOWLEDGMENTS

If anything emerges from this book's mistakes, it is thanks to generous readings by Stephanie Ford, Kate Colby, Kate Schapira, Ryan Flaherty, GC Waldrep, Josh Edwards, and the Canarium Books editors.

Thanks also for support &/or wildly inspiring presences to: Matt Hart, Brigit Pegeen Kelly, David Markson, Nate Pritts, Justin Quarry, Megan Snydercamp, Katie Umans, Bill Walsh, Charlie White, Dean Young, Ellen Litman, Charles Mahoney, Penelope Pelizzon, Roger Wilkenfeld, Liz Howort, my wonderful students, the University of Connecticut, Bread Loaf Writers' Conference, the Poetry Society of America, the Greenhills Visiting Writer Fellowship, and the Rhode Island State Council of the Arts; the editors at *Absent*, *BOMBLOG*, *Barrow Street*, *Forklift Ohio*, *The Nation*, *Pool*, *West Branch online*, *Handsome*, *Ocean State Review*, *MiPoesias*, *Missouri Review online*, and the *RE:Telling* anthology; my family; and, profoundly, C.